The WORLD
CREATED,
FALLEN,
REDEEMED,
and
RESTORED

The Gospel Plan of God

Written by **Sally Michael**
Illustrations by **Fred Apps**

The World Created, Fallen, Redeemed, and Restored: The Gospel Plan of God

Copyright © 2019 by Next Generation Resources, Inc. Illustrations by Truth78.

All rights reserved. No part of this publication may be reproduced in any form without written permission from Truth78.

Published in United States of America by Truth78.

All Scripture quotations, unless otherwise noted, are from the ESV® Bible (The Holy Bible, English Standard Version®) copyright © 2011 by Crossway, a publishing ministry of Good News Publishers. Used by permission. All rights reserved. ESV Text Edition: 2016.

ISBN: 978-0-9969869-9-1

Truth:78 / Equipping the Next Generations
to Know, Honor and Treasure God

Truth78.org · info@Truth78.org · 877.400.1414 · @Truth78org

Dedicated to Brian and Cindy Eaton.

*You were **created** in God's image,*
*separated from your Creator as an inheritor of the **fallen** nature of Adam,*
***redeemed** by the precious sacrifice of Christ's death on the cross,*
and one day will be restored in glory!

Your friendship is a precious gift from God.
Your partnership in ministry is a continual encouragement.
And your love for the Gospel is a blessing that refreshes the soul.

May all your children
—Joe, Natalie, Mariah, Isaiah, and Grace—
join you at the marriage feast of the Lamb.

A Note to Parents:

Children need to understand the big picture story of the Bible. Many children come to believe that the Bible is a collection of disconnected stories that have little relation to each other—Noah and the ark, Moses and the burning bush, David and Goliath, and so on. The Bible itself does not present its teaching to us as disconnected stories, but rather tells us a unified and interconnected story that stretches from the very beginning of creation to a new heaven and a new earth.

It would be pedagogically unwise to rush to Jesus and the cross when teaching children the story of the Bible, even though Jesus' work of redemption is central to Scripture's unified message. Children need to appreciate the significance of the one true God and His work of creation. They need to contemplate the pervasive impact of the fall upon the hearts and lives of men. The form of Scripture's canonical presentation of unfolding truths should impact how we present Scripture's teaching to children. Scriptural teaching to children should be systematic, and build chronologically and conceptually upon itself, precept upon precept.

Within the pages of this book we cannot give your child the full understanding he would gain from being taught the whole counsel of God, but we can acquaint your child with the four major narrative points or plot movements of the Bible—creation, fall, redemption, and restoration. This will serve as a framework on which your child can begin to build an understanding of the parts of the Bible.

Here are a few suggestions for you to consider as you read this book:

- Read at your child's pace. This may require reading the book in more than one sitting, depending on your child's ability to concentrate, understand, and be engaged.
- Dialogue with your child as you read.
- Reinforce the four major themes of creation, fall, redemption, and restoration.
- You may want to pause and sing or listen to a suggested hymn or worship song. You need not sing the whole song.
- Verses requiring varying cognitive ability are used to explain each of the major themes. You may want to read all or part of the verses. It may be necessary to explain words your child does not understand.
- Consider memorizing the suggested verses.
- Pray that God will open his eyes and heart as you read the book with your child.

May your child see the beauty and majesty of God, the reality and horror of his sin, the amazing grace of Jesus' sacrifice on the cross, and the sure hope of eternal life and indestructible joy in God.

CREATION

In the beginning, God created the heavens and the earth... And God saw everything that he had made, and behold, it was very good.—*Genesis 1:1, 31a*

Let all the earth fear the LORD; let all the inhabitants of the world stand in awe of him! For he spoke, and it came to be; he commanded, and it stood firm.—*Psalm 33:8-9*

How did this world begin?

It began with the one true God,
the Ruler of all things. He just spoke
with His almighty voice and made
the whole world—day and night,
sky and sea, land and plants. He
made the sun, the moon and
stars. All of it was good,
and all of it shows
God's greatness
and goodness.

But God didn't stop there.

God's greatness and goodness just kept flowing out to create fish and birds and all kinds of animals.

Can you name some of them?

God saw all that He had made, and it was good.

..."I am the LORD
who made all things,
who alone stretched out the heavens,
who spread out the earth by myself,"
—Isaiah 44:24b

How many are your works, O LORD!
In wisdom you made them all;
—Psalm 104:24a, NIV 1984

And then God made His most special creation of all.

This creation would be different from all the others. It would be made in God's likeness or image. Unlike the rest of creation, this creation would be able to enjoy loving relationships and think and create in ways like God.

This creation would be a reflection of God's holiness and goodness. It would show God's goodness and greatness in a very different way from all the rest of creation. God did more than speak this time when He created. He took special care in this, His most special creation.

...then the LORD God formed the man of dust from the ground and breathed into his nostrils the breath of life, and the man became a living creature.—*Genesis 2:7*

God planted a garden for the man, Adam, to live in and care for. In the garden were all kinds of beautiful plants and trees with delicious fruits, nuts, leaves, stems, roots and seeds to eat...and God gave all of them to Adam to use and enjoy except one tree, the tree of the knowledge of good and evil. God gave Adam a very important warning about this tree. God was not only his Creator, Ruler, and Friend but also the One who knew what was best for man.

And the LORD God commanded the man saying, "You may surely eat of every tree of the garden, but of the tree of the knowledge of good and evil you shall not eat, for in the day that you eat of it you shall surely die."

—Genesis 2:16-17

God is loving and generous. He gave Adam every kind of food he needed. He told Adam how to live in joy and how to care for the world. He warned Adam of danger. What does this tell you about God?

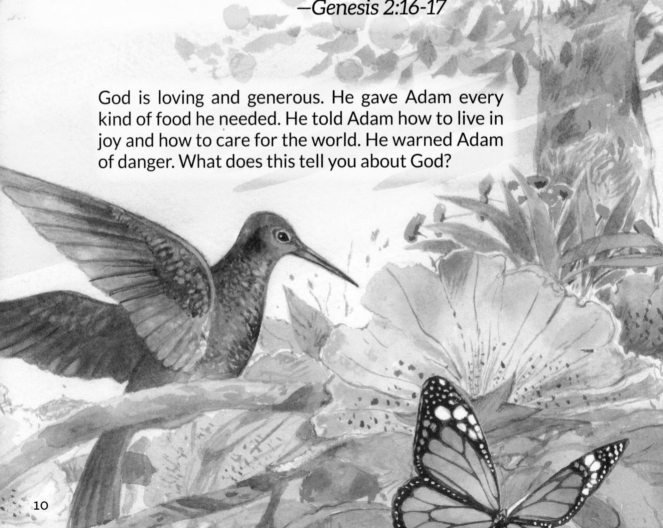

10

When God created Adam, He was not done doing good and showing His greatness and worth. And God was not done showing His care and kindness to the man.

Then the LORD God said, "It is not good that the man should be alone; I will make him a helper fit for him."... So the LORD God caused a deep sleep to fall upon the man, and while he slept took one of his ribs and closed up its place with flesh. And the rib that the LORD God had taken from the man he made into a woman and brought her to the man.—*Genesis 2:18, 21-22*

So God created man in his own image,
in the image of God he created him;
male and female he created them.—*Genesis 1:27*

Adam and Eve were made to love, trust, and obey God. They were made to honor, thank, and enjoy God—to show that God is most special of all. They were made to see His greatness and worth, and to find their greatest joy in knowing God.

Adam and Eve lived in a perfect world—a world where there was no sickness, no evil, and no unkindness. There was no anger, no sadness, and no loneliness. But most of all, this world was perfect because Adam and Eve got to be with God in the garden, talk with Him, and enjoy happy friendship with Him.

Would you like to live in a world like that?

What would it be like to live there?

Optional Activity: *On the internet, look up and listen to the song Indescribable by Chris Tomlin. Think about the greatness of God as you listen.*

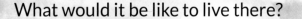

FALL

For what can be known about God is plain to them, because God has shown it to them. For his invisible attributes, namely, his eternal power and divine nature, have been clearly perceived, ever since the creation of the world, in the things that have been made. So they are without excuse. For although they knew God, they did not honor him as God or give thanks to him, but they became futile in their thinking, and their foolish hearts were darkened.—*Romans 1:19-21*

Adam and Eve could see the greatness and goodness of God in the world around them. They saw the strength of the elephants and the majesty of the soaring birds. They tasted the sweetness of fruit and felt the warmth of the sun. They walked and talked with God in sweet friendship with Him.

But sadly, this was not enough for them. They were not satisfied with God's protection, care, and friendship. They wanted to be independent and trust themselves rather than God. They wanted to be the most important and most special. They did not believe God's words or trust that He is good.

Though they were made to honor, love, and obey God, and to trust that He knows what is best for them, Adam and Eve were foolish and turned away from God. They reached out...and took the forbidden fruit from the tree of the knowledge of good and evil. First Eve took and ate it. Then she gave it to Adam, who also disobeyed God and ate it.

When God came walking in the garden, Adam and Eve did not come toward Him... Instead they ran away from Him and hid. But no one can hide from God who knows all things...and no one can rebel or turn against God and disobey Him without consequences.

This is what the Bible tells us about God:

You who are of purer eyes than to see evil and cannot look at wrong,—*Habakkuk 1:13a*

When Adam and Eve disobeyed God's command, they also broke their relationship with God. Because of their sinful hearts, they could no longer be near a pure God. Adam and Eve could no longer live in the garden and walk as friends of the perfect and holy God. Their lives would now be full of pain and difficulty.

God is right to punish sin. He has the authority or right to decide on the punishment for sin. God's punishment for sin is death, just as He had warned Adam when He told Adam not to eat the fruit. And, just like God said it would, death entered this perfect world because of sin. From now on, there would be suffering, anger, and hatred...rebellion, envy, and selfishness.

Adam and Eve now had a sin problem. But God is merciful and kind, and He made a way to cover Adam's and Eve's shame. God Himself made clothes for Adam and Eve with animal skins. What had to happen to the animals to get the skins?

Death had now come into the world. Things would always be different from now on. The perfect creation was now groaning with brokenness and sin. Would it be this way forever?

Because of man's disobedience, sin would spread from Adam to all his children and their children and their children...to all people in all times.

Therefore, just as sin came into the world through one man, and death through sin, and so death spread to all men because all sinned—*Romans 5:12*

We do not reflect or show the beauty and perfection of God the way we were created by God to do. We were made to show that God is loving, good, faithful, and right in all He is and does. Instead, we show that our hearts are selfish, unkind, disobedient, rebellious, unfaithful, prideful, and envious. Have you ever been selfish or unkind or disobedient? What does that mean for you?

No one is free from sin. Everyone has a sin problem that separates us from a holy and perfect God.

...for all have sinned and fall short of the glory of God,—*Romans 3:23*

Year after year, evil has spread through every person because every person has been infected with sin. God's goodness and greatness can still be seen in creation...but that creation is now also scarred with sin, suffering, pain, and all kinds of evil. What evil do you see in the world today?

We cannot fix the evil and brokenness in this world. We cannot fix our sinful hearts. Is there any way to be rescued or saved from our sinful hearts and the suffering of this world? How can we be acceptable to a holy God? How can we honor Him, love Him, and obey Him? How can we live in joy, peace, goodness, and perfect love forever? Is there any hope for us?

After Adam and Eve sinned, God not only covered their sin and shame, He also gave

a PROMISE.

God would send a Savior, Someone to take the punishment for man's sin forever, to make things right again and fix all that is wrong in the world and in man's heart...

Someone who would crush evil.

REDEMPTION

He himself bore our sins in his body on the tree, that we might die to sin and live to righteousness.—*1 Peter 2:24a*

For as by the one man's disobedience the many were made sinners, so by the one man's obedience the many will be made righteous.—*Romans 5:19*

We cannot fix our sin problem, or be acceptable to a good and holy God, or live again in a perfect world. We do not find our greatest joy in God, and honor, love, and obey Him. But God can solve our sin problem...and only God can. God is all-powerful, always good, full of kindness to undeserving sinners, and wise. To fix the sin problem, God would use another garden and another tree. But first, God had to do an act of amazing love and sacrifice.

God sent His Son, Jesus, into the world to become a man. Jesus left heaven, a place of perfect love, peace, and goodness to be born as a baby into this sinful, broken world.

This was God's plan from the beginning to save man from sin and punishment. Unlike Adam and Eve, and all people, Jesus lived a life of perfect sinlessness, reflecting the goodness, greatness, and loving heart of God the Father.

Jesus came to show us who God is...
to show us the perfect love, faithfulness, power, and forgiveness of God.

Jesus healed sick people—attacking the curse of sin. He made lame people walk again and blind people see.

He showed the power of God by commanding storms to be still and by multiplying two fish and five loaves of bread to feed a crowd of 5,000 people. He did things that only God can do...because

Jesus is God.

He preached and taught about the consequences of sin, and the need to turn away from sin and turn to God. He taught about the beauty of God's ways, like repaying good for evil and forgiving each other. He promised that His Father was preparing a home in heaven for those who would trust in Him, where they could live forever with God. Man could once again be in wonderful friendship with God, and walk and talk with Him again. What does this tell you about God?

But someone had to pay for the sins of man for all God's promises to come true...and that Someone was Jesus. Jesus knew He would need to bear God's anger and punishment for sin. He would have to die a bloody, agonizing death to save man. God would turn away from Jesus and let Him experience the worst kind of death, and pain, and sorrow there ever could be.

Would Jesus finish the plan of God? Would He die for sinful men? Jesus went to another garden...the Garden of Gethsemane. He needed to talk to God the Father. He fell on His face and prayed.

"My Father, if it be possible, let this cup pass from me; nevertheless, not as I will, but as you will."—*Matthew 26:39b*

Jesus knew He would experience intense suffering on the cross, but in perfect obedience to God He was willing to die for our sin. He was willing to be the once for all time, forever payment for sin. Jesus was willing to take the punishment for His people so we could receive God's love and forgiveness.

Even though Jesus never did anything wrong, soldiers came and arrested Him.

They beat Him, made fun of Him, and put a crown of sharp thorns on His head. Then Jesus carried the beam of a cross on his back... a beam made from the wood of another tree.

On a hill called Calvary, Jesus was nailed to a cross and was left to suffer and die.

He could have called an army of angels to rescue Him. He could have freed Himself from the cross and put to death those who hated Him...but He didn't. Instead, He stayed on the cross. He died to take away sin and give His perfect righteousness (obedience) to everyone who would trust in Him.

29

Later, he was laid in a cave-like tomb.
The Savior was dead.

How could a dead Savior save the world?
Was there any hope for sinful man?

Yes, there was hope! Three days later God raised Jesus from the dead just as He had planned! Jesus didn't stay dead! He showed His power over death and sin! He spoke to His friends. He showed them the scars from the nails in His hands. He ate with them. And He spoke of a better Kingdom to come...the Kingdom of God.

Then, Jesus was taken up to heaven to sit at the right hand of God the Father. God made a way for all who believe in Jesus—for all those who trust in Him to be their Savior, King, and Friend—to be forgiven of sin and receive the promise of eternal life in Heaven.

For the wages of sin is death, but the free gift of God is eternal life in Christ Jesus our Lord.—*Romans 6:23*

Optional Activity: *On the internet, look up and listen to the song Stronger by Ben Fielding and Reuben Morgan. (We particularly appreciate the version done by Christ's Community Church, published on October 5, 2013.) Think about what Jesus did to break the curse of sin. You could also find and listen to The Wonderful Cross by Chris Tomlin. (We particularly appreciate the version published by First United Methodist Church of Luling, Texas on March 7, 2015.) Why is the cross— a place of suffering and pain—wonderful? Think about the contrasts in this song: richest gain being loss, sorrow and love, die to find life.*

RESTORATION

"In my Father's house are many rooms. If it were not so, would I have told you that I go to prepare a place for you? And if I go and prepare a place for you, I will come again and will take you to myself, that where I am you may be also."—*John 14:2-3*

But God, being rich in mercy, because of the great love with which he loved us, even when we were dead in our trespasses, made us alive together with Christ—by grace you have been saved—and raised us up with him and seated us with him in the heavenly places in Christ Jesus, so that in the coming ages he might show the immeasurable riches of his grace in kindness toward us in Christ Jesus.—*Ephesians 2:4-7*

Jesus promised to return again someday. He will come to put an end to sin forever and to make all things new again. How will Jesus do this?

Jesus will come this time, not as a baby but as a king...as the King of Kings! He will come with power and justice to judge sin and evil and to make a new heaven and a new earth. The Bible says Jesus will judge all men. Just like Adam and Eve could not hide from God, no one will be able to hide from Jesus, the King of Kings. Those who have not turned from sin, trusted in Jesus, and lived to honor, love, and obey Him will be condemned forever. They will suffer eternal punishment and pain. Those who have trusted in Jesus, turned from sin, and lived in trust and obedience to His ways, will live forever with God.

This is what the Bible tells us about the new heaven and the new earth:

Then I saw a new heaven and a new earth, for the first heaven and the first earth had passed away, and the sea was no more. And I saw the holy city, new Jerusalem, coming down out of heaven from God, prepared as a bride adorned for her husband. And I heard a loud voice from the throne saying, "Behold, the dwelling place of God is with man. He will dwell with them, and they will be his people, and God himself will be with them as their God. He will wipe away every tear from their eyes, and death shall be no more, neither shall there be mourning, nor crying, nor pain anymore, for the former things have passed away."—*Revelation 21:1-4*

But nothing unclean will ever enter it, nor anyone who does what is detestable or false, but only those who are written in the Lamb's book of life.—*Revelation 21:27*

Where will you stand on that day? Will you be with those who are trusting in Jesus...living forever with Jesus in His perfect heaven?

Or will you be with those who have gone their own way in rebellion against God, trusting in themselves...receiving eternal punishment and suffering?

Jesus' death on the cross is good news for sinners! He offers forgiveness, peace, life eternal...and indestructible joy—joy that can never be destroyed or taken away! All this He offers us as a free gift!

For by grace you have been saved through faith. And this is not your own doing; it is the gift of God, not a result of works so that no one may boast.—*Ephesians 2:8-9*

Do you want to love, honor, and thank God? Do you want to find your greatest joy in knowing God? Do you want to trust in Jesus and enjoy Him forever? This is the promise Jesus has made:

"All that the Father gives me will come to me, and whoever comes to me I will never cast out." —*John 6:37*

Optional Activity: *On the internet, look up and listen to the song I Can Only Imagine by Bart Millard. What do you think it would be like to see Jesus for the first time? What would you feel and think?*

REVIEW THE GOOD NEWS!

You have just finished reading about the greatest, best, most powerful news in the whole universe! It is the most important news ever given to men, women, and children because it is found in God's true Word, the Bible. It is the only news that can bring you true happiness that will last forever. This good news is, "There is salvation in Jesus alone! Trust in Him and you will be saved!"

 ## CREATION
God created all things, and it was good. God created man to love, honor, obey, and give thanks to Him—and to show that He is most special of all by enjoying Him (Psalm 33:8-9).

 ## FALL
Adam and Eve foolishly turned away from God and disobeyed God, bringing sin, death, and all kinds of evil into God's good world. Through Adam, sin spread to all men, causing a separation between God and man (Romans 1:21; Romans 3:23).

 ## REDEMPTION
God sent His Son, Jesus, to die on the cross to receive the punishment sinners deserve. Jesus rose from the dead and is now in heaven. Through trusting in Jesus, sinners can be forgiven of sin and receive His perfect righteousness and the promise of eternal life (1 Peter 2:24).

 ## RESTORATION
Jesus will return as the victorious King of Kings to put an end to sin forever and make all things new. Jesus will also judge every person. Those who have not trusted in Him will be condemned forever. But those who have trusted in Him will live joyfully forever with God (John 14:2-3).

SHARE THE GOOD NEWS!

Who could you share this news with? Use the pictures and words above to help you tell someone about the good news of Jesus.

RECOMMENDED RESOURCES

Helping Children to Understand the Gospel
A booklet that covers preparing the hearts of children to hear the Gospel, discerning stages of spiritual growth, communicating the essential truths of the Gospel, and presenting the Gospel in an accurate and child-friendly manner. Includes a 10-week family devotional.

Glorious God, Glorious Gospel (Devotional, Coloring Book, Notebook)
A family devotional for parents to use with their children to ground them in the essential, foundational, and glorious truths of the Gospel. Accompanying notebooks and coloring books are also available to engage and equip young minds.

Making HIM Known Series
The Making HIM Known series (*God's Names*, *God's Promise*, etc.) was written to give parents an opportunity to present solid truth to their children, and to encourage real-life application of the truth. The books include devotions, activities, follow-up questions, and application.

Mothers: Disciplers of the Next Generations
This booklet challenges moms to look on their mothering with a biblical perspective, to daily seize opportunities to encourage faith in their children, and to rely on Him to accomplish the great work to which He has called moms.

A Father's Guide to Blessing His Children (Book and App)
Pronouncing blessings upon our children is a powerful way to plead for God's grace upon them and give them a vision for what we hope they will become. The booklet, *A Father's Guide to Blessing His Children*, and the app, *A Father's Blessing*, can help you establish and sustain a regular pattern for blessing your children (and others) that will encourage and strengthen their faith.

Fighter Verses™
The Fighter Verses Program is designed to encourage believers to fight the fight of faith through memorizing God's Word. Each week individuals, families, and churches are all encouraged to memorize a verse or short passage of Scripture together.

Big, Bold, Biblical Prayers for the Next Generation
David Michael casts a vision for how and why we need to pray big, bold, biblical prayers, and provides 17 prayers you can join him in praying for the next generation, along with relevant Scripture passages to spark your prayers.

To order these and other discipleship resources, visit Truth78.org/products

Truth:78 / Equipping the Next Generations to Know, Honor, and Treasure God

Truth78 is a vision-oriented ministry for the next generations—that they may know, honor, and treasure God, setting their hope in Christ alone, so that they will live as faithful disciples for the glory of God.

Our mission is to nurture the faith of the next generations by equipping the church and home with resources and training that instruct the mind, engage the heart, and influence the will through proclaiming the whole counsel of God.

We are committed to developing resources and training that are God-centered, Bible-saturated, Gospel-focused, Christ-exalting, Spirit-dependent, doctrinally grounded, and discipleship-oriented.

RESOURCES AND TRAINING MATERIALS

Truth78 currently offers the following categories of resources and training materials:

VISION-CASTING AND TRAINING

We offer a wide variety of booklets, video and audio seminars, articles, and other practical training resources that highlight and further expound our vision, mission, and values, as well as our educational philosophy and methodology. Many of these resources are freely distributed through our website. These resources and trainings serve to assist ministry leaders, volunteers, and parents in implementing Truth78's vision and mission in their churches and homes.

CURRICULUM

We publish materials designed for formal Bible instruction. The scope and sequence of these materials reflects our commitment to teach children and youth the whole counsel of God over the course of their education. Materials include curricula for Sunday School, Midweek Bible programs, Backyard Bible Clubs or Vacation Bible School, and Intergenerational studies. Most of these materials can be adapted for use in Christian schools and education in the home.

PARENTING AND FAMILY DISCIPLESHIP

We have produced a variety of materials and training resources designed to help parents disciple their children. These include booklets, video presentations, family devotionals, children's books, articles, and other recommended resources. Furthermore, many of our curricula include Growing in Faith Together (GIFT) Pages to help parents apply what is taught in the classroom to their child's daily experience in order to nurture faith.

BIBLE MEMORY

Our Fighter Verses™ Bible memory program is designed to encourage churches, families, and individuals in the lifelong practice and love of Bible memory. The Fighter Verses program utilizes an easy-to-use Bible memory system with carefully chosen verses to help fight the fight of faith. For pre-readers, Foundation Verses features 76 key verses with simple images. Visit FighterVerses.com for weekly devotions and free memory aids. Download the Fighter Verses App for quizzes, songs, devotionals, review reminders, and other helps.

For more information on any of these resources and training materials contact:

Truth78.org · info@Truth78.org · 877.400.1414 · @Truth78org